THE SPIRIT OF
THE UPANISHADS

THE SPIRIT OF THE UPANISHADS

OR

THE APHORISMS OF THE WISE

A Collection of Texts, Aphorisms, Sayings, Proverbs, Etc., from "The Upanishads," or Sacred Writings of India, Compiled and Adapted from over Fifty Authorities, Expressing the Cream of the Hindu Philosophical Thought.

YOGI RAMACHARAKA,

WILLIAM WALKER ATKINSON

GYAN

Published by

Gyan Publishing House
5, Ansari Road
Daryaganj, New Delhi-110002
Phone: 011-47034999, 9811692060
E-mail: books@gyanbooks.com

Distribution Network
gyanbooks.com
India, USA, Canada, UK, Australia

ISBN: 978-93-6208-552-8 (HB)
First Published, 1907

2nd Impression 2024

Printed at: Gyan Press, Delhi.

THE SPIRIT OF THE UPANISHADS
Author: YOGI RAMACHARAKA, WILLIAM WALKER ATKINSON

THE UPANISHADS

THE SPIRIT OF

THE UPANISHADS

OR

THE APHORISMS OF THE WISE

A Collection of Texts, Aphorisms, Sayings, Proverbs, Etc., from "The Upanishads," or Sacred Writings of India, Compiled and Adapted from over Fifty Authorities, Expressing the Cream of the Hindu Philosophical Thought.

"*Hear thou even the little child, and from his words accept thou the Truth that goeth straight to thy heart. But reject all that doth not so go to thy heart—no matter how high the authority—yea, even though the lotus-born creator, Brahm, himself, be the speaker.*"—YOGAVASISHTHA.

THE YOGI PUBLICATION SOCIETY

CHICAGO, ILL., U. S. A.

CONTENTS

PREFACE.

This volume is a collection of texts; aphorisms, sayings; proverbs; etc., from *"The Upanishads,"* or Sacred Writings of India; compiled and adapted from over fifty authorities, expressing the Cream of the Hindu Philosophical Thought.

The adapter of the book acknowledges his appreciation of the work of Dr. Manil N. Dvivedi, of Bombay, India, the original translator of many of these aphorisms, etc., the general form of whose translation has been followed in the majority of cases, subject to such supplementary changes and rearrangement as have seemed desirable in the present work.

The contents of this book are self-explanatory, and need little introduction. The wonderful philosophy of *"The Upanishads,"* is so generally recognized that words of praise would be superfluous. Many can say with the German philosopher, *Schopenhauer:* "In the whole world there is no study so beneficial and so elevating as that of *'The Upanishads.'* It has been the solace of my life; it will be the solace of my death."

One word of caution we would give to the reader who may not be grounded in the fundamental thought of the Hindu Philosophies. We allude to the frequent use of the words: "The Self," or "Self," in many of the aphorisms. The student of the Oriental Teachings will, of course, recognize the fact that the word "Self," so used, implies the "One Self," or "Infinite One," whose Essence permeates the Universe, and in whom all living forms, "live, and move and have their being"—and which "Self" is the Essence of the countless *personal* "selves." We have used the Capital "S," in the word, when so used; the word "self," meaning the personal self, being printed in the usual way.

The thought and teachings underlying this entire book, is that of this ONE SELF—the only REALITY. The personal self is a thing of the moment—being born; growing old; and dying—but the Real Self, endureth forever. The Real Self, in each of us, is the SPIRIT in each of us, which is at One with the Father. Nearly every aphorism in the book emphasizes this Truth, in various words and forms of expression, and many of them are intended to lead the reader to a Realization of The Truth.

Some of these seed-thoughts will appeal to one, and others to another—each will draw to himself that which is his, and will let the rest pass him by. This is the Law of Learning: *Accept only that which appeals to your Heart, as Truth—let the rest pass you by, for the time being —for to each comes his own; and none can gain his own, until he is prepared for it.* The words of the *Yogavasishtha,* quoted on our title page, intended to convey this same truth. Listen to this Aphorism of the Wise:

"Hear thou even the little child, and from his words accept thou that Truth that goeth straight to thy heart. But reject all that doth not so go to thy heart as Truth—no matter how high the authority—yea, even though the lotus-born creator, Brahma, himself, be the speaker."

Therefore, accept the pearl of Truth, even though it lie in the mud of the gutter—and reject that which does not seem to be the real Truth, even though it be offered you from the hand of one of the gods. Test all statement of Truth, by the light of the Spirit within you, and you can not stray far from The Path.

We would call the attention of our readers, to the edition of "*The Bhagavad Gita,*" or "Message of the Master," published simultaneously with the present volume. This first mentioned book, should be read by all who enjoy the present one, for it contains the key to the Higher Teachings, which the writers of these Aphorisms wished to express.

We trust that this little book will cause the minds of many to unfold to the light.

THE YOGI PUBLICATION SOCIETY.

CHICAGO, ILL., U. S. A., January 12, 1907.

The Spirit of The Upanishads.

PART I.

THE THRESHOLD.

That wherein disappears the whole of that which affects the mind, and that which is also the background of all;—to THAT I bow,—the all eternal consciousness, the witness of all exhibitions of the Intellect.

Upadesasahasri.

As is the sight of the sweetest Honey to the traveller in the Desert, so is the perception of the ever-effulgent.

Brhadaranyakopanishad.

I expound in half a verse what has been told in a million volumes;—THAT is the Truth, the world is illusion. the soul is none other than THAT.

Upadesasahasri.

Action leads to incarnation, and incarnation to pleasure and pain. Hence arise all likes and dislikes which again propel to action resulting in merit and demerit. These put the ignorant wanderer, again, into the bonds of incarnation;—and so on and on, for ever, rolls the wheel of this world. Nothing but ignorance is the cause of all this; the remedy lies in the destruction of ignorance. Knowledge of *Brahman* is the way to find final beatitude in the destruction of this ignorance. For knowledge alone, not action which is only a part of ignorance, is competent to accomplish this result. Nor is it possible to do away with likes and dislikes so long as ignorance is not done away with. This is therefore undertaken with the object of destroying ignorance as well as its effects—this world,—and also of explaining the real philosophy of *Brahman*.

Upadesasahasri

From the senses finding each its own gratification in the objects peculiar to each, there arises no real happiness, but only a temporary allaying of the fever of the mind. It is vain, therefore, to grope for any real happiness in the world of objects. The deluded deceive themselves by imagining every experience of evil to be so much good; but in birth, death, and limitation, the wise never fail to perceive the evil that conceals itself under the inviting form of objects. They find no happiness in things subject to such results. The smallest happiness, in the real sense of the word, is no way possible in any thing;—oh! I should become that Self which is all bliss, all existence, all enlightenment.

Atmapurana.

Knowledge of the Divine dissolves all bonds, and gives freedom from every kind of misery including birth and death.

S'vetasvataropanishad.

The Creator (*Brahma*), the Protector (*Vishnu*), the Destroyer (*Siva*); the Consumer, the Sun, the Moon, the Thunder, the Wind, the Sacrifice, and so on, are terms used by the sages to describe the One Eternal, as they look at It through the multifarious forms of the intellect;—all my best worship to that Divine Essence, the destroyer of that ignorance whose form is this world.

S'ankaracharya.

PART II.

THE ABSOLUTE.

That should be known as *Brahman*, which, beyond the gaining whereof, there remains nothing to gain; beyond the bliss whereof there remains no possibility of bliss; beyond the sight whereof there remains nothing to see; beyond becoming which there remains nothing to become; beyond knowing which there remains nothing to know.

Atmabodha.

This is All, and so is that;—All comes out of the All,—taking away the All from the All, the All remains for ever.

Isopanishad.

He is eternal among the eternal, conscious among the conscious; He, ever one, produces the variety of ideas in the many;—knowing that Divine One, as the Supreme Cause, all bonds dissolve themselves into nothing.

S'vetasvataropanishad.

THAT which, in the beginning, sent forth the Creator (*Brahma*) and favoured him with the storehouse of all knowledge, the *Veda;*—I, desirous of liberation, betake myself to It, the ever-effulgent light, revealing Its eternal Self through the intellect.

S'vetasvataropanishad.

As in the sun, all light, there is neither day nor night, so in The Absolute, all light, there is neither knowledge nor ignorance.

Upadesasahasri.

The ever unchangeable is devoid of sound, touch, form, taste or smell. It is without beginning or end, ever beyond the prime cause of all evolution;—knowing that, one escapes the all-devouring jaws of death.

Kathopanishad.

The eye has no access there, nor has speech nor mind; we do not know It (The Absolute), nor the method whereby we can impart It. It is other than the known as well as the unknown; so indeed do we hear from the sages of old who explained It thus to us.

Kenopanishad.

Try to realize (within thyself) THAT whence arise these beings, by which they stand sustained, and unto which they return and become naught;—that indeed is The Absolute.

Taittiriyopanishad.

To the emperor (Janaka) thus explained *Yajnavalkya;*—When there is, *as it were*, a second, there alone does one see, smell or taste something other (than Self); there alone does one speak to or hear, think of or touch or know something other (than Self). But when the seer is all alone with THAT, he is as still as an undisturbed body of water,—this indeed is Spiritual Consciousness, the condition of universal empire. This to the self, is the highest end, the best riches, the supremest world, the greatest joy;—the rest of beings live only by a particle of this bliss.

Brhadaranyakopanishad.

Father, son, mother, nay even the worlds, the Gods, the *Vedas* are all naught in The Absolute; the thief is no-thief, the ascetic no-ascetic;—It has no relation with good or evil. One who has become It is beyond all desires of the heart. It should not be supposed that (even in sleep) It does not see, for It does not see though ever seeing; the sight of the seer is never lost, being eternal, there is nothing other than Itself which It can make the object of Its seeing.

Brhadaranyakopanishad.

The Absolute is described as "not this," "not that," and so on by negatives only.

Brhadarnyakopanishad.

That is real bliss which has no conditions; in the conditioned there can be no happiness;—the Unconditioned alone is bliss; try to realize the Unconditioned (in thyself.)

Chhandogyopanishad.

That is the Unconditioned wherein one does not see another, one does not hear another, one does not know another; that wherein one sees another, hears another, knows another, is the Conditioned. The Unconditioned is immortal. the conditioned is mortal. Oh master! where is this Unconditioned to be found? Everywhere or nowhere!

Chhandogyopanishad.

Hence is described the Real Self; This Self alone stands above, below, west. east. south and north: everywhere all is this Self. He who thus sees, thinks and knows, enjoys this Self, plays with this Self, has this Self alone even for a second, finds perfect bliss in this Self, becomes the lord of all, gains access to all worlds and beings. Those who understand otherwise, betake themselves to other masters, enjoy only the mortal world of conditions, find no access to all beings and all worlds.

Chhandogyopanishad.

THAT which is ever awake even in sleep, sending forth the variety of ideas, is the Real Self, and all immortality;—all the worlds are held in it (as it were, in suspension), there is nothing which transcends it. It is this. As the *one* fire pervading the universe *appears* in so many forms in the variety of objects, so the Inner Self of all, ever one, appears to take on so many forms, but it is ever beyond them. As the sun who enlightens everything has nothing whatever to do with the numerous ills the eye may perceive, so the Inner Self of all, ever one, has no connection whatever with the joys and sorrows of the world, being ever beyond them.

Kathopanishad.

THAT is the real Witness, all consciousness, who unites in one grasp, the actor, act and the variety of objects apart one from the other. I see, hear, smell, taste and touch,—in this form does the Witness unite all in one continuous consciousness, even like the lamp suspended in a theatre. The lamp in the theatre takes in the master, the audience, the actors and all, without distinction, in one sweep of light, and continues to shed the same light even when all these are not there.

Panchadasi.

The Seer of thy sight thou shalt not see; the Hearer of thy ear thou shalt not hear; the Thinker of thy thoughts thou shalt not think; the Knower of thy knowledge thou shalt not know—this is thy Real Self, all-pervading, everything besides is but mortal.

Brhadaranyakopanishad.

Without the glass there is no possibility of a sight of the reflection; whence then could there be any possibility of the knowledge of *name* and *forms* without assuming that which is Existence, Consciousness, and Bliss?

Panchadasi.

He pervades the earth and yet transcends it; the earth knows Him not; the earth is His body: He controls the earth from within;—He is thy inner Self ever immortal. He pervades water and yet transcends it; water knows Him not; water is His body: He controls water from within;—He is thy inner Self ever immortal. * * * * He is the unseen Seer; the unheard Hearer; the unthought Thinker; the unknown Knower. There is no Seer other than this; no Hearer other than this; no Thinker other than this; no Knower other than this. THAT is thy inner self, ever immortal; all besides is mortal.

Brhadaranyakopanishad.

THAT which is not spoken in speech but that whereby all speech is spoken. THAT which does not think in the mind but that whereby the mind proceeds to think. THAT which does not perceive with the eye but that whereby the eye receives its sight. THAT which does not hear with the ear but that whereby the ear hears. THAT which does not breathe the breath of life but that whereby life itself is kept up. Know thou that THAT is The Absolute, not this that people worship.

Kenopanishad.

Immortal Spirit alone is THAT; the east, west, south and north is all THAT: This wide expanse of the universe above and below is indeed all THAT.

Mundakopanishad.

In the beginning, oh good one! was The Absolute alone; all one without a second.

Chhandagyopanishad.

Brahma, Indra, Prajapati, all the gods, the five primordial elements, and all that breathes, or moves about, or flies above, or stands unmoved,—the whole universe exists through Thought, depends on Thought, Thought is its stay;—the Thought of the Absolute.

Aitareyopanishad.

This Real Self is all intellect, all mind, all life, all eyes, all ears, all earth, all water, all wind, all ether, all light, all darkness, all desires, all peacefulness, all anger, all quiet, all religious merit, all religious demerit; It is the All, It is this, It is THAT.

Brhadaranyakopanishad.

This Real Self is causeless, without a second, having no within and without; this Self is The Absolute, the consciousness of all.

Brhadaranyakopanishad.

Oh Gargi! this immutable one is the unseen Seer, the unheard Hearer, the unthought Thinker, the unknown Knower;—There is no Seer beside this; no Hearer beside this; no Thinker; no Knower beside this. In this immutable Essence, oh dear Gargi! is interwoven the essence of all existence.

Brhadaranyakopanishad.

He (Yajnavalkya) said, oh Gargi! the knowers of The Absolute thus explain the ever Immutable. It is neither with dimensions nor atomic, neither short nor long; It is not red, not sticky, not light, not dark; neither air, nor ether. It has no relation, no taste, no smell, no eye, no ear, no speech, no mind, no light, no life, no mouth, no form, no break, no without;—It enjoys nothing or is enjoyed by nothing.

Brhadaranyakopanishad.

Objects transcend the senses; the mind transcends objects; the intellect transcends the mind; the *mahat* (*i. e.* cosmic consciousness) transcends intellect (*i. e.* individual intellect); the *avyakta* (*i. e.* the undifferenced first cause), transcends the *mahat;* the Real Self transcends the *avyakta;*—beyond the Real Self there is nothing which can transcend It, or prevent It from being the last essence, the last resort of all.

Kathopanishad.

That is the Great Real Self who, though without hands or feet, is the swiftest of approach; though without eyes or ears, sees and hears everything; though uncomprehended, comprehends everything knowable.

S'vetasvataropanishad.

The Absolute is never born, never dead. It comes out of nothing and goes into nothing.—It is unborn, eternal, immutable, ever unique, never destroyed with the destruction of the body. If the killer intends to kill, or if the killed thinks He is killed, both of them do not *Know;* they neither kill nor are killed. It is smaller than an atom, greater than the universe. It is present in the heart of all beings. The glory of this Self is realized by him the whole of whose sensibility returns to a state of placid calmness through absence of desire;—he alone passes to the other side of this ocean of sin and sorrow.

Kathopanishad.

Truth alone conquers, not falsehood, the divine path stands upheld by Truth; sages with desires put out by satiety pass over it to the great treasure of Truth. It (the Truth) is all-embracing yet unthinkable, all light, minutest of the minute yet ever manifest. It is farthest of all yet ever near in all beings, ever present in the hidden consciousness of all which passes out in all acts of mind and body.

Mundakopanishad.

One so freed from the bondage of senses transcends all material relation, and becoming all supreme light, regains his own Self. This indeed is Self. It is beyond mortality, beyond fear, It is Truth;—Truth is only another name of The Absolute.

Chhandogyopanishad.

There cannot be any room for separateness in that intransmutable, formless, characterless, Absolute Being which is beyond the relations of subject, object, instrument, etc., which is every way full to the utmost, like the waters surging above all things at the great cyclic deluge. In it merges the cause of illusion like darkness in light;—there, verily, can be nothing like separateness in It, the highest Essence, without character, and ever one without a second.

Vivekachudamani.

THAT is the form of the highest Self wherein the world of subject and object though existing does not exist, and which though all *akasa* has no touch with it. It is all void and yet as if it were no void, the world is naught in it, it continues to be completely void though full of numberless worlds upon worlds.

Yogavasishtha.

The whole of this cosmos is One Self, there is no room for the idea of body and its like. THAT is all that is, all bliss, whatever thou seest is all thought.

Yogavasishtha.

As light belongs to the sun, coldness to water, and heat to fire, so do existence, consciousness, bliss, eternity, immutable purity, belong by nature, to THAT.

Atmabodha.

The material cause of this illusion is none other than THAT; the whole of the universe is, therefore, THAT, and nothing else. THAT being the All, causality is mere illusion;—the real Truth being thus known there can be no room for the slightest separateness.

Aparokshanubhuti.

This Real Self is the bridge, the support, of the whole universe which, but for it, will be nowhere.

Chhandogyopanishad.

THAT is all bliss of every kind; Attaining this bliss one realizes his nature which is all bliss.

Taittiriyopanishad.

THAT therefore is the last measure of all bliss.

Taittiriyopanishad.

The one ever-effulgent stands concealed in all beings. It pervades every knowable object and is the Inner Self of all. It is the witness of all action, the all-embracing resort of beings, the unaffected seer, all thought, unique, and without properties.

S'vetasvataropanishad.

It has neither form nor instruments. It is not seen as equal to or greater than any thing. Its transcendent power is heard of as unimaginably multifarious, omniscience and omnipotence constitute Its very nature.

S'vetasvataropanishad.

It is unborn, ever awake, free from dream, having no form or no name. It is one continuous thought, all-knowing. There is no metaphor whatever in saying this.

Gaudapadacharya.

This oh Satyakama is THAT higher as well as lower. Science and nescience all is THAT.

Prasnopanishad.

As above so below. as below so above; he passes from death to death who here finds the least shadow of variety. There is no variety in THAT. It should be grasped by the mind alone. He, indeed, passes from death to death who here finds the least shadow of variety.

Kathopanishad.

As a hawk or an eagle having soared high in the air, wings its way back to its resting-place, being so far fatigued, so does the soul, having experienced the phenomenal, return into Itself where it can sleep beyond all desires, beyond all dreams.

Brhadaranyakopanishad.

The sun does not shine there nor the moon nor the stars nor even these lightnings, least of all this fire; everything becomes enlightened in its light, the whole of this shines through Its lustre.

Kathopanishad.

PART III.

THE REAL SELF.

A particle of Its bliss supplies the bliss of the whole universe, everything becomes enlightened in Its light; nay all else appears worthless after a sight of that essence; —I am indeed of this Supreme Eternal Self.

Vijnananauka.

The power of sun, moon, fire and even of speech having exhausted itself; the senses being all extinguished. THAT which stands self-illumined, beyond all relations, sending forth this universe of ideas, and all thought, is shown to be the Inner Self of all.

Svarajyasiddhi.

I am without character, without action, without imagination, without relation, without change, without form, without sin, all eternity, ever liberated.

Atmabodha.

If thou objectest "how I should grasp this?" Pray do not grasp it,; for the *residuum* after all grasping is at end, is none other than thy Real Self.

Panchadasi.

Where is the man who doubts the fact of his own existence? If such a one be found, he should be told that he himself, who thus doubts is the Self he denies.

Svatmanirupana.

No other knowledge is necessary in *knowing* ones self, for the Self is all knowledge;—the lamp requires not the light of another lamp for its own illumination.

Atmabodha.

Setting aside every thing which becomes the object of knowledge in this world, there yet remains a residuum, the real essence of knowledge. The knowledge that this is the Real Self, is true knowledge of the Self.

Panchadasi.

It is the ear of ears, the mind of minds, the speech of speech, the breath of breaths, the eye of eyes. The wise transcending these (*i. e.* the physical ear, mind, etc.) and renouncing this world of experience, rest in eternal immortality.

Kenopanishad.

This Self in my heart is smaller than a grain of rice or barley or mustard, smaller than a grain of the *Syamaka* or even than a part of its part. And yet, this Self in my heart is bigger than the earth, more extensive than the atmosphere, wider than the sky, greater than all these worlds together. It is all action, all desire, all smell, all taste; It pervades all that is; It is void of speech, and all other senses; ever indifferent to good or evil. This indeed is the Self in my heart, this indeed is the Real Self. He becomes this Real Self, after passing away from here, who has faith in the Self, and has no doubt whatever.

Chhandogyopanishad.

All this is the One Self, this Self is the Universal Self.

Mandukyopanishad.

As the fool with eyes all bedimmed, sees the sun all dark, though covered only with a cloud, so does It appear in bondage only to the victims of illusion. I am this pure Self whose form is all eternal consciousness.

Hastamalakastotra.

It is the one pervading all, but ever untouched by any, and therefore ever pure, and all clear, like the all-pervading *Akasa*. I am this pure Self whose form is all eternal consciousness.

Hastamalakastotra.

It is without mind, without eyes, without any similar means of relating itself to the objective. But nevertheless, it is the mind as well as the eye of all minds and all eyes, nay the means of means;—Its form being ever incomprehensible by the mind, the eyes and the rest. I am this pure Self, all eternal consciousness.

Hastamalakastotra.

I am indeed that Supreme eternal Real Self which is all bliss; all light; beyond illusion; beyond conditions; realizable only in the idea "I AM."

Vijnananauka.

It is this infinite atom, all this is that Self from end to end, It is the Truth, It is the Self;—oh S'vetaketu! THOU ART THAT.

Chhandogyopanishad.

As a lump of salt melted in water cannot be experienced by the eye, but only by the tongue, so indeed the ever-existent Real Self shining in the depth of the heart, cannot be realized by the external senses, but only by the light of that sympathetic awakening which comes from the word of a teacher. THOU indeed ART this REAL SELF, not the phenomenal that appears around.

Svarajyasiddhi.

The ocean transformed, through the action of clouds, into the form of rivers, etc., ceases to be itself; so indeed hast thou forgotten thyself through the power of conditions. Oh friend! remember thy full Self, THOU ART THE REAL SELF,—the ground of existence—the ALL.

Svarajyasiddhi.

Where there is anything like duality there alone does one see another; there alone does one smell another; there alone does one hear another; there alone does one speak to another; there alone does one think of another; there alone does one know another. But when all is One

Self to him, what should he smell, and with what? what should he see, and with what? what should he hear, and with what? what should he speak of, and with what? what should he think of, and with what? what should he know, and with what? By what indeed should that be known through, which knows everything? By what should the Knower be known?

Brhadaranyakopanishad.

It is not attainable by the most constant attendance at lectures. For many, though hearing numerous such, never know what It is. Strange indeed is the speaker who speaks of It; stranger still who obtains It; but most strange of all is he who, being properly instructed by a competent teacher realizes It in himself and all.

Kathopanishad.

PART IV.

THE WAY.

Till study should not allay in thee the sense of separateness, the mind cannot take on the form of that essence, and thou canst not realize The Real Self. Four indeed are the gatekeepers at the entrance of the palace of liberation:—(1) Self-restraint, (2) Contemplation, (3) Contentment, (4) Company of the Wise.

Yogavasishtha.

He alone escapes from the web of illusion in this world, (even like the lord of beasts from the trap which holds him fast,) who, with all acts, all pleasures, attuned to the Supreme Aim, puts forth strong personal effort in that behalf.

Yogavasishtha.

Trees continue to vegetate, and so do live on beasts and birds; he alone *lives* whose mind lives *not* in consequence of taking on a variety of forms. All holy writ is so much burden to him who has no discrimination, all philosophy is so much burden to him whose germ of desire is not destroyed; the mind is so much burden to him who has not acquired self-control, the body is so much burden to him who knows only the *anatman* (non-self.)

Yogavasishtha.

There can be no man more despicable than him who does not put into practice the words of the proficient teacher, who explains, with great pains, the Real Truth, on being questioned.

Yogavasishtha.

All desire is ignorance, the destruction of desire is liberation, and this liberation oh Rama! is easily brought about only by ceasing to desire. The mind experiences bondage from the firm conviction "I am not the Real Self." It realizes entire freedom, from the equally firm conviction "I am the Real Self."

Yogavasishtha.

He continually sees the Real Self, who studies to unify philosophy, and the teacher's explanations, with the facts of his own consciousness.

Yogavasishtha.

The light breaking in upon the mind should not be excluded by that false logic which puts forth unholy guesses of every kind up to the obliteration even of the facts of consciousness.

Yogavasishtha.

With no confidence in the facts of his own consciousness, and with the obvious endlessness of argumentation, how would he who poses himself as a Professor of Logic, obtain conviction of Truth? If argumentation is meant as a help to the intellect, you are welcome to argue in accord with the facts of your consciousness, but certainly not to argue without aim, in any line you choose.

Panchadasi.

The sense of this can never be gathered by Intellect alone, oh beloved one! it leads to real knowledge only when used by one who really knows. This knowing is that which thou, oh child of truth! hast already acquired; —oh *Nachiketas!* there indeed can be no better questioner than Thyself.

Kathopanishad.

This Self is not realizable by study, nay not even by intelligence or much learning. The Self unfolds its full essence to him alone who applies his self to Self. He who has not given up the ways of vice, he who is not able to control himself, he who is not at peace within, he whose mind is not at rest, can never realize the self, though full of all the learning in the world. That which lies at the root of all distinctions of caste and creed is its food, even death itself is its drink;—who, not so prepared, can know what It is?

Kathopanishad.

How can books enlighten that lump of clay fashioned in the form of man, who does not in any manner realize the Truth explained to him with all possible clearness.

Naishkarmyasiddhi.

We rejoice with those whom we recognize as centered in Self Realization; the rest we pity; with the deluded we do not care to argue.

Panchadasi.

Talk as much philosophy as you please, worship as many gods as you like, observe all ceremonies, sing devoted praises of any number of deities;—liberation never comes, even at the end of a hundred *kalpas*, without realization of the Oneness of Self.

Vivekachudamani.

Who knows Spiritual Consciousness passes beyond death, and enters Immortality.

Isopanishad.

The Good is one thing, the Agreeable another; men find them in a variety of objects and become bound, one way or other. He who attaches himself to the Supreme Good reaps the highest bliss; he who persues the Agreeable is cheated of the real object of existence.

Kathopanishad.

These, the Good and the Agreeable, thou knowest, are opposed one to the other in their very nature, and having entirely different results in store. Oh *Nachiketas!* the various desires I propose to thee fail to move, thou art really devoted to the Agreeable alone. Groping about in its night, fools flatter themselves with wisdom and learning, and continue to tumble about, without end, like the blind led by the blind.

Kathopanishad; Mundakopanishad.

The lyre with all the beauty of its make, and the melody of its music, serves at best to please the hearer; it cannot lead to universal empire. In the same manner all the flow of speech, all the stream of sweet words, all the skill expended in explaining philosophy,—all that the learned call learning, has the senses and mind, not the Self, for its end. Vain is the study of philosophy if it leads not to the Essence, equally vain is all philosophy if the Essence is realized.

Vivekachudamani.

Disease disappears not with the mere name of medicine, but by actually swallowing it. Talking of the Self, without proper realization, can never bring about liberation. Till the objective is not dissolved in the subject; till the Essence of Self is not realized; no liberation can come from speaking Its mere name—all the fruit of such, activity is only waste of so much breath.

Vivekachudamani.

PART V.

THE STUDENT.

The knowing intellect skilled in grasping the *pros* and *cons* of every theme, and cleared of all dross by the means just described, is the true aspirant after self-knowledge. Discrimination, non-attachment, self-control and its accompaniments, keen desire of liberation, these make one fit to inquire after The Real Self.

Vivekachudamani.

This Self cannot be realized by want of spiritual strength, by indifference, by austerities unaccompanied with renunciation. The self of that knower who applies himself to Self with the means described enters the Great Self. Sages having found It, stand ever content in Spiritual Consciousness; remain centered in the Self, being free from all attachment, and always at peace within and without. They find the unconditioned and all-pervading, and realizing It within, become one with the All. With faith firmly fixed in the teaching of the *Yogis*, with the mind entirely purified through renunciation and Spiritual Consciousness, ascetics, one with the immortal, become one with the Real Self at the moment of dissolution.

Mundakopanishad.

In the air or in water no mark is seen of the passage of birds or fishes; so is entirely inscrutable the passage of the knowers of the Self.

Sankaracharya.

The eye perceives not sound, being dissimilar by nature; the material eye cannot see the spiritual self.

Naishkarmyasiddhi.

As the face is fully reflected in a clear glass, so in the true seeker the Spirit is reflected in the intellect.

Atmapurana.

He *knows* who finds a teacher; he then delays only so long as he is not free from the body, for on being so free he is one with the All.

Chhandogyopanishad.

Having obtained this priceless birth, with all the senses in their full activity, he who does not understand the good of Self, destroys himself.

Mahabharata.

The boat—this body—has been chartered by thee at the heaviest price—all thy good acts —to cross over to the other side of this ocean of sin and sorrow. Pray pass on before it breaks.

Miscellaneous.

Those who destroy their Self, go, after death, to the sphere called *Asurya* (without the sun), all enveloped in thick darkness.

Isopanishad; Brhadaranyakopanishad.

PART VI.

THE TEACHER.

Till thy mind reaches the stage of intuitive development, follow what is assured thee by teachers, books and the logical instruments of knowledge. When thus is burnt out all latent desire, and the Thing is realized, thou shouldst not hesitate to give up all concern even with these, however good or useful they be.

Yogavashitha.

By my book is meant all that is written by way of explaining the facts of nature, by great souls free from likes and dislikes, with eyes trained to observation and reason. Those resolute souls who are full of the highest goodness, who are equal to all, and who are possessed of a tact peculiar to themselves, are the really wise.

Yogavasishtha.

I, thus informed, am yet only versed in the words of the *Mantras* (the sacred hymns), I know nothing of Self. I have heard from sages of your stamp that the knower of Self rises above all sorrow. With all my learning, I am full of discontent and sorrow, oh Lord! take me to the other side of this ocean of misery.

Chhandogyopanishad.

This Real Self should be explained by the father to his eldest son, or by the teacher to a properly sympathetic pupil, and to no one else.

Chhandogyopanishad.

Oh *Rama!* the cause of Self-Realization is none other than the pupil's own intelligence.

Yogavasishtha.

One course leads to success in one birth or many, by gradual practice after the manner pointed out by the teacher; the other leads soon to real Spiritual Consciousness through the Self, aided even by intellectual development, even like the fall of the fruit from above.

Yogavasishtha.

Having supported Self by Self, of one's own accord, through *reflection*, one should carry this deer—his own mind—across the ocean of delusion, this world.

Yogavasishtha.

Tell me what thou seest as other than religion and non-religion, other than these effects or their causes, other than that which is past and that which is yet to come.

Kathopanishad.

S'aunaka, the rich householder, approached *Angirasa* in due formality, and asked oh Lord! Teach me that whose knowledge leads to the knowledge of all that is!

Mundakopanishad.

The ultimate aim of all the *Vedas*, the final result of all austerity, the object of keeping the period of studentship, I describe to thee in brief:—it is the syllable "AUM." This is the symbol of the immutable self; this is the highest Essence. It becomes whatever he desires to him who knows this, the ever-unchangeable. This, indeed, is the highest support, the greatest help, betaking himself to this he becomes glorified in THAT.

Kathopanishad.

The knower of *the Self* attains to the Supreme; hence it is said "*The Self* is Being, Consciousness, Limitlessness." He who realizes this, present in the intellect, as well as in the highest *Akasa*, has access to the fruition of all desire whatever, at one sweep, being one with all-seeing Self.

Taittiriyopanishad.

This cosmos is all *Soul;* all ceremonial; all austerities; the highest immortal *Self.* He who realizes this in the cavity of the heart, easily scatters into nothing, oh good one! the knot of *Illusion*, even in this life.

Mundakopanishad.

The wise knowing, through the practice of subjective concentration, the All-effulgent One, extremely difficult to see; concealed deep beyond everything; shining through all acts in every heart; inaccessible; and without beginning; they transcend all pleasure and all pain.

Kathopanishad.

He who sees himself in All, and All in himself, attains to the empire of Self, thus worshipping Self and looking on all things with equal eye.

Manu.

Knowing the great all-pervading Self, through whom is experienced the whole of dream and waking, the wise never become subject to sorrow.

Kathopanishad.

As surely as water showered on a table-land seeks the lower ground, so indeed does one seeing variety in the attributes of Personality, become attached to them in future. As water poured upon a clear even surface stands ever pure and undefiled, so stands the Self of the silent *knower*.

Kathopanishad.

This body is the city, with nine gates, wherein dwells the unborn, unfailing Consciousness. He who knows this well never comes to grief, and is liberated twice over.

Kathopanishad.

These rivers flowing to and gaining the ocean lose themselves in it, lose even their name and form, and become included in the name "Ocean." So do all the sixteen forms of the objective flowing to and gaining the Self become lost in Him. They lose even their name and form, and become included in the Self. This Self is the immortal, transcending all forms of the mortal. This is thus summed up:—That death may not overpower thee, know the only knowable, the Self, in whom are centred all forms like the radii of a chariot-wheel in its hub.

Prasnopanishad.

Know that one Self alone with which are bound sky, earth, atmosphere, mind, and all the vital breaths. Leave aside all other speech. This alone is the bridge over the gulf of this world to Immortality.

Mundakopanishad.

The *Brahmans* disown him who knows other than Self as a *Brahman*. The *Kshatriyas* disown him who knows other than Self as a *Kshatriya*. The people disown him who knows other than Self as the people. The gods disown him who knows other than Self as a god. The spirits disown him who knows other than self as a spirit. Everything disowns that which knows other than Self as the thing. The *Brahmans;* the *Kshatriyas;* the people; the gods; the spirits; everything;—is Self.

Brhadaranyakopanishad.

That Self which is beyond sin, decay, death, sorrow; which requires no food nor drink; which is all accomplished desire, all fulfilled thought; should be looked for, should be inquired after. He gains access to all worlds, has all his desires fulfilled, who, having known this Self, realizes It fully in himself and all.

Chhandogyopanishad.

Said *Yajnavalkya* to the Emperor *Janaka:* The same has been explained by the *Vedas* as well: this, indeed, is the eternal glory of him who has realized The Absolute. It neither grows nor is diminished by doing, or not doing, any act. The knower *knows* this very truth. Knowing this, he is not affected by any *Karma* whatever, all being as sin to him. The heat of his senses cools down into that calmness of mind which follows on absence of desire; All kind of latent attachment leaves him; No conditions disturb him; Ecstasy environs him,— who knowing thus sees Self in Self, sees the All as Self. No good or evil touches him; he transcends all good and all evil. The fulfilment or non-fulfilment of any secular or temporal act affects him not, he having reduced them all to nothing. He is beyond all form; beyond all desire; beyond all doubt. This is the real Spiritual Consciousness, this is the real condition of Spirit.

Brhadaranyakopanishad.

I know this Self to be the All, the Great Self, all effulgence, transcending all darkness. Knowing this, one can transcend even death;—there surely is no other road out of this world.

S'vetasvataropanishad.

Like and dislike do not cease to affect him who yet relates himself to the body; these never touch him who has disembodied himself, mentally.

Chhandogyopanishad.

As oil is found in *sesamum*-seeds; as *ghee* is found in curds; as water is found in water-courses; or as fire is found in the *arani*-wood: so is the Self seen in Self by him who tries to realize It through universal love and perfect control over mind and body.

S'vetasvataropanishad.

Brahmans and others desirous of knowing It, know It by the study of the *Vedas;* by sacrifice: by ascetic practices unaccompanied with desire;—knowing It they become the Silent Ones.

Brhadaranyakopanishad.

Having explained the *Vedas* to his pupil, the teacher thus enjoins him: Tell the truth; go by religious forms; never disregard thy proper study; and having satisfied thy teacher do not put an end to thy line.

Taittiriyopanishad.

Three are the stays of religion:—Sacrifice, Study, and Charity.

Chhandogyopanishad.

He who knows It the immutable Spirit thus; and he who does not know It thus; both perform *Karma* by It. Wisdom and Ignorance admit of innumerable varieties; that alone which is done with knowledge, faith, and complete surrender, becomes powerful for good.

Chhandogyopanishad.

Even like the radii fixed in the hub of a chariot-wheel, is He, the Eternal one, pervading everything, and appearing as many, after the forms of the intellect. Meditate on this thy Self as the syllable *Aum.* May you be ever happy in the realization of THAT which transcends all darkness.

Mundakopanishad.

Seeing the whole universe subject to the law of causation, the *Brahmans* understands that there is nothing other than the Self which is the causeless uncreate, and finding no use in acting up to the ideals of the world feels supreme contempt for everything. He then repairs, with holy grass in hand, to the teacher, well-versed in sacred lore and full of the realization of Spirit, to inquire after the Eternal. The knower explains to him, who with mind free from all egoism, and with the senses turned within, repairs to him, thus questioning, that Inner Doctrine which reveals the eternal Self, the highest Truth.

Mundakopanishad.

The chief help to self-realization is, however, that reflection which comes of one's own effort. All the rest, including the teacher's grace, and so forth, are but subordinate means to the end. Attend, therefore, carefully to the principal means.

Yogavasishtha.

PART VII.

THE LESSON.

Beyond desire; without parts; above egoism; being or non-being;—whatever Thou art, Thou canst not escape from being the Self. Thou destroyest; protectest; givest; shinest; speakest; though ever free from egoism; —wonderful is the power of *Maya*, illusion.

Yogavasishtha.

He thought: I may become many and multiply. He objectified himself and evolved all this, everything whatever. Having evolved this, he entered into it; and entering became all positives and all negatives, all spirit and all matter, all infinite and all finite.

Taittiriyopanishad.

Then, when It was all Unmanifest, It, of itself, became manifest through name and form, endowing everything with this or that name, and this or that form. All things even till now are defined by some name and some form. This is all the import of Its entering in the objective evolved from itself.

Brhadaranyakopanishad.

Dadhyangatharvana thus described this "Divine Honey" to the *Asvinikumaras;* the seer telling what he saw, describing It as taking on a separate form with every form. The ever-effulgent is understood to take on many forms through illusion solely for the purpose of self-realization.

Brhadaranyakopanishad.

The one who is self-enlightened, becomes everything from the highest to the lowest; becomes the many in dreams, and as it were, enjoys all pleasures, laughs a hearty laugh with friends, or feels the sense of fear on seeing cause for it.

Brhadaranyakopanishad.

In dreams there are in reality no chariots; no horses, not even the course on which the chariot may run; and yet all these are mentally created in a moment. There are in reality no joys; no pleasures; no delights; and yet all are mentally seen and felt at the instant. There are in reality no ponds, no lakes, no rivers; and yet all are there at the merest thought. This power of evolving any number of forms from Itself is the Creative Power of the One.

Brahadaranyakopanishad.

This, therefore, is the Truth. As from fire well lighted, fiery sparks flow off in all directions by the thousand, so do all beings of every variety come out, oh good one! from the ever Immutable, and are resolved also into the same. It is the self-illumined, formless, *Spirit*, all within and all without; unborn; without breath; without mind; above all conditions; beyond the eternal cause of the phenomenal.

Mundakopanishad.

Camphor and the like never cease to emit fragrance, though kept in any place whatever. The whole of the phenomenal may, in the same manner, be seen in that which is all consciousness. As the bracelet is in the gold; as water is in the mirage, or even as a wall stands round the city seen in dream; so subsists the form of every object in the subject.

Yogavasishtha.

He who generally knows everything, knows the same particularly also; this omniscience is the only austerity known to him.

Mundakopanishad.

As the statue pre-exists in the wood; and a statue

exists again in every limb of that statue; and so on *ad infinitum*, so does this gigantic statue—the Kosmos—exist in the One.

Yogavasishtha.

The wise realize everywhere THAT which is beyond sight; beyond grasp; which has no relation whatever; which has no form; which has no eye and no ear, no hand, no foot; which is eternal, all-pervading, smallest of the small, ever immutable, the source of all being. As a spider spins out his web from within himself and draws it in at pleasure; or as herbs grow out of the earth; or as hairs grow out of the living man, so, indeed, does evolve the Kosmos from the ever unchangeable One.

Mundakopanishad.

This *Asvattha*-tree, with root upward and branches extending below, stands eternally thriving; it is the spotless, it is as the Self, that verily is the Immortal; all worlds subsist in it, nothing can transcend It. This is THAT. Through It burn fire; through It shines the sun; through It thunders *Indra;* through It blows the wind. If thou failest in this world to see the Light before the dissolution of thy body, thou hast before thee a passage in another body through worlds and creations.

Kathopanishad.

As consciousness bears witness to itself, or as separateness bears out separateness, so is illusion sufficient, of itself, to bear out itself and everything in contains. This indeed is Illusion, capable of bringing about things and events beyond conception;—it deludes all in the whirl of its illusive action.

Svarajyasiddhi.

The Self-Existent inflicted a curse on the senses in endowing them with a tendency to objectivize; it is hence that they tend to objects without, and not to the subject within. Some rare Sages desirous of immortality see the Self, turning their eyes within. Children find pleasure in the objective, and become bound in the expansive net of death; the wise knowing immortality as the only thing stable, care not to desire anything of the impermanent.

Kathopanishad.

Self is the rider on the chariot of this body guided by the intellect as charioteer, drawn by the senses as powerful horses, controlled by way of the mind serving for the reins. Thus runs the vehicle over the course of experience. The Self thus conditioned by the senses and the mind is called the Enjoyer by those who know. He who is forsaken by the charioteer (intelligent discrimination), and has no idea of guiding the reins—his mind—in the proper manner, has no control over the senses, and is like a driver of restive horses. He who has the intellect for his driver and the mind for proper reins, is able to reach the other end of the course, the highest essence of the All-Pervading. THAT ever concealed in all, is never manifest, but is grasped by the sharp intellect of those who are trained to minute observation.

Kathopanishad.

Though having only three *Gunas*, or Qualities, Thou art the cause of all the worlds; even the gods fail, through want of insight, to measure the depth of Thy immeasurable power. Thou art the sustainer of all, the whole of this universe is only a particle of Thyself;—thou indeed art the undifferentiated first cause, the highest *Prakrti.* Oh Divine Mother! thou art that supreme science of power inconceivably immense, which sages desirous of liberation, rising above every weakness, apply themselves to, with the inner power of their senses held tight in perfect control.

The Saptasati (Markendeyapurana).

Thou art the light that shines through the sun, dispelling the darkness of ignorance prevailing within; thou art the vein that carries the fragrant honey of the flower of consciousness to every particle of matter; thou art that which becomes thousands of that jewel which satisfies every desire of the needy; thou, Divine One! art to those struggling in the ocean of incarnation, the Restorer and Preserver.

Anandalahari.

This divine godess, the power of supreme illusion forcibly drags away the mind even of the knower into the web of delusion.

Saptasati (*Markandeyapurana*).

He who while fully attached of his body, desires to realize Self, prepares to cross a river on the back of a crocodile mistaking it for a piece of wood.

Vivekachudamani.

If the Wise Man leans towards objects and enjoyments, forgetfulness throws him off the guard, like an adulteress her paramour, by clouding his intellect. As moss moved from upon the face of water stands not away even for a minute, delusion (*Maya*) envelopes even the knowing one, if he is off his guard.

Vivekachudamani.

A woman may appear as a wife, daughter-in-law, sister-in-law, brother's-wife, mother, and so on, respectively, to the several persons related to her, but she herself continues ever one.

Panchadasi.

That the origin of experience is explained from evolution, after the manner of pots, etc., from clay; instruments etc., from iron; or sparks from fire; is only a method of putting the matter to the learner; there is, in reality, no distinction whatever in the All.

Gaudapadacharya.

He, who imagines a limit in the limitless, transcendant, Self, has, of himself, put his self in bondage.

Yogavasishtha.

That which is naught at beginning and end, is naught

in the present moment also; things though fully resembling unreality, are said to be real by a kind of metaphor.

Gaudapadacharya.

Experience known as *experience* tends to degrade, but known as import of the World, it becomes all perfect bliss.

Yogavasishtha.

Thou alone eternally evolvest through the gracefulness of thyself made up of being and non-being, having for its embodiment the wonderful variety of endless objects.

Yogavasishtha.

As the rope, not understood as such, is mistaken, in the dark, for a snake, so is Spirit mistaken for the variety of this world.

Gaudapadacharya.

Experience, full of likes and dislikes, is verily a dream; real while it lasts, all unreal on being awake.

Atmabodha.

PART VIII.

THE LAW OF KARMA.

Fortitude, forbearance, self-restraint, no desire for other's wealth, purity, control over the senses, conscious intelligence, spiritual culture, truthfulness, absence of anger,—these ten make up the characteristics of all true religion whatever.

Manu.

As the caterpillar, getting to the end of the straw, takes itself away after finding a resting-place in advance, so the Soul leaving this body, and finding another place in advance, takes himself off from his original abode. As the goldsmith taking little by little of the gold expands it into a new form, so, indeed, does this Soul, leaving this body, make a new and happy abode for himself.

Brhadaranyakopanishad.

The sacrifice of the ignorant drowns itself and those who betake themselves to it. Those fools who imagine any good in this, are led again and again into the wheel of decay and death. Those men of stupid intellect who imagine vain forms and ceremonies as the height of religion, and know no good besides, return again into this world or even into a lower one.

Mundakopanishad.

Therefore, as here, in this world, dies out what may be encompassed by *Action*, so dies out in the world next to this, all that may be acquired through acts of formal religion.

Chhandogyopanishad.

Forms of religion but forge so many bonds round the individual; Spiritual Consciousness alone disperses them.

Maha-Bharata.

Formal religion has its use in purification of the intellect, it cannot show us THAT. THAT is realized through reflection, not at all even by a million forms of worship.

Vivekachudamani.

Karma leads to that result alone which it can produce, reach, evolve, or modify; liberation is not brought about in any of these ways; hence *Karma* cannot be the means of liberation.

Naishkarmyasiddhi.

Karma never dispels ignorance, being under the same category. Knowledge alone destroys ignorance, even as light dispels darkness.

Atmabodha.

Happiness or misery is not in any one's giving, it is all a misunderstanding of the intellect which shows either the one or the other as coming from some one else. Nay, the proud egoism even in the act, of the form "I do it," is entirely vain. Every individual is governed by *his own Karma.*

Miscellaneous.

PART IX.

DEVOTIONAL WORSHIP.

All this verily is the Self, for it is *of* it, *in* it, and *through* it. The self-controlled should devote himself to this Self. The man is all Idea, whatever Idea the man cherishes in this world that he becomes in the next. Fix thyself, therefore, on to the Idea of the Self.

Chhandogyopanishad.

Teachers; interpretations of sacred texts; the force of religious merit; none of these lead to the realization of THAT which is revealed in the clear reflection of the heart, engendered from contact with the good.

Yogavasishtha.

Clarified butter, though present in every part of the cow, conduces naught to her nourishment. It serves as the best nourishment to its producer, only when worked out into its proper form. In the same manner, the highest effulgent Self, present in all beings, even like the clarified butter, is never of any practical use to them, till properly realized through the force of devotion.

Yogavasishtha.

If you ask what can be the difference between Spiritual Consciousness and devotion? pray hear; reflection is bound up with the *thing*, devotion with the *actor*. Spiritual Consciousness comes cf reflection, no opposite desire can put it out; it burns up every appearance of reality in the world of phenomena, in the very moment of its birth.

Panchadasi.

This body is the holy *Kasi;* the river of Spirituality flowing through and through the three worlds is the sacred

Ganges; devotion and faith stand for the heavenly *Gaya;* the much-coveted *Prayaga* is, indeed, in deep concentration at the feet of the teacher; and this inner Self, the fourth, the witness of every one's mind, is the God;—if thus all holy places stand together in this body of mine, what other place could be holier to seek?

Kasi-panchaka.

Formal objects of worship are devised for the use of those who have not yet realized the Essence; going by miles is devised for those who cannot go by leagues.

Yogavasishtha.

Said *Prajapati:* whence does come this fear! With the thought, "why did I fear?" disappeareth all fear; for, fear comes of duality.

Brhadaranyakopanishad.

Insist not on the order of steps in the process of Self-realization; the inverted vision which, like hunger, is the cause of much tangible suffering, must in one way or other, be cured.

Panchadasi.

Attend to this, the essence of all Spirituality, and attending, digest it well. Desire alone is bondage, its destruction is liberation.

Yogavasishtha.

To all ascetics whatever, the condition of Fearlessness depends upon control of the mind, which leads also to destruction of misery; perfect light, and inexhaustible peace.

Gaudapadacharya.

The mind of *Rama!* is that which is between being and non-being, which stands between spirit and matter, which in fact swings to and fro between the two.

Yogavasishtha.

Thinking evolves the objective. All the three worlds

exist in and through thinking. The Kosmos melts away on its dissolution. This thinking should carefully be diagnosed.

Yogavasishtha.

All ideas come of Thinking, they disappear on suspension of Thinking. Attune this Thinking, therefore, to the highest Self, thy Inner Consciousness.

Vivekachudamani.

That which leads to false vision, sets up the *Personal Self* in place of *the Real Self;* shadows forth a thing in nothing;—this oh *Raghava!* is that which we describe as "thinking."

Yogavasishtha.

Abandon all latent desire for the multitude of enjoyments pressing round. Nay give up even the desire for life as represented in the body. And finally rise above all sense of being and non-being. Find thus full Bliss in absolute Spiritual Knowing.

Yogavasishtha.

My mind was occupied elsewhere, and I did not see; my mind was occupied elsewhere, and I did not hear; it is through the mind alone that one sees or hears. Love, thought, doubt, belief, unbelief, patience, impatience, intelligence, shame, fear, all make up the mind.

Brhadaranyakopanishad.

Mind alone is, to men, the cause of bondage or liberation;—lost in the enjoyment it leads to bondage, emptied of the personal it leads to liberation.

Panchadasi.

The light of *Spirituality* breaks not in full force upon that puny thing which is all beclouded with fear of the world, with pride of learning; and with love of life.

Smrti.

The father, being victim of Illusion, bewails the loss of

his son, taking him for dead, though he be full of life in some far off land. On the other hand, he does not bewail even though his son be dead, till the information has reached him. It is plain, the cause of bondage lies in the *mental creation.*

Panchadasi.

You may drink the ocean dry; you may uproot from its base the mountain *Meru;* you may swallow fire. But more difficult than all these, oh Good One! is control over the mind.

Panchadasi.

As fire, not fed by fuel, subsides into its place, so, indeed, does all thinking die out into its source, on not being led into modifications of any kind.

Jivanmuktiviveka.

He who understanding the mind applies himself, again and again, to subduing it, gains no success without the help of some consummate plan, even like one who fails to subdue a mad elephant without the iron hook. Application to spiritual science; company of the good; abandonment of latent desire; restraining the flow of breath; these are some of the most useful means to control the mind. Those who, in face of these, try to control it through physical practices, lose sight of the lamp, while vainly dispelling darkness with darkness.

Yogavasishtha.

Renounce all conformity with the world, give up all concern of the body, nay, have nothing to do with the forms of religion and learning;—thus wear off the false illusion that wraps thy-Self.

Vivekachudamani.

As one desirous of coming out successful in debate applies himself closely to the study of poems, plays, logic and the like, so must he who desires liberation *reflect* constantly on himself.

Panchadasi.

The God of the twice-born is Fire. The God of the Silent one is his Heart. Poor intellects find their God in idols. The even-eyed enlightened one sees God *everywhere.*

Uttaragita.

PART X.

FREEDOM.

That mean spirit should be avoided from a distance, who, relying on the unseen Fate, attributes his conduct to the unreal and false idea of some one necessitating it from behind. He is verily a beast, constantly in another's power, who thinks he goes to heaven or hell as God may will it.

Yogavasishtha.

Even the body being of illusion, where could there be any room for necessity? That the *Vedas* speak of necessity is only for the enlightenment of the ignorant.

Aparokshanubhuti.

In this world, oh child of the *Raghus!* every one can always compass everything through well-directed personal effort.

Yogavasishtha.

Resort to personal effort. Hear such word of scripture as points out some useful line of action. The rest, even though as old as time, should be overlooked, with the eye fixed on truth and truth alone.

Yogavasishtha.

The wise, relying on necessity, should not give up free personal effort, for even necessity works through freedom.

Yogavasishtha.

He who sets himself not at liberty by cutting the tight bond—his mind—with his mind, can never be freed by any one else.

Yogavasishtha.

PART XI.

SPIRITUAL KNOWING.

Spiritual Knowing, is of all means, the only direct means of liberation. Liberation is never accomplished without it, as sure as food is not cooked without fire.

Atmabodha.

The Real Truth is seen by *reflection* engendered through some beneficent suggestion; it can never be seen by constant washing, by giving gifts, nay not even by a hundred breathing exercises.

Vivekachudamani.

The state of the Real Self is within reach of those alone who are full of austerity, virtue, and truthfulness. Those, indeed, find that entirely pure condition, in whom there is not the remotest trace of fashionable lies or deliberate falsehoods, nor any hypocrisy whatever.

Prasnopanishad.

When entirely disappear all desires rankling in the heart, the moral becomes immortal, and fully realizes *the Self* even here. When here, indeed, burst all ties that bind the heart so fast, the mortal surely becomes immortal. This verily is the teaching of the whole of the *Vedanta.*

Kathopanishad.

No means other than *reflection* can produce real Spiritual Knowing. Nothing but light can ever reveal the existence of things.

Aparokshanubhuti.

Reflection may run as follows:—Who am I? How is this evolved? Who can be the creator of this? What may be the material cause? And it may proceed to answer the questions thus:—I am not the body—a mere cluster of elements,— nor even the senses. I am something quite different from the one as well as the other. Things come out of ignorance, but die away on the rise of Spiritual Knowing.

Aparokshanubhuti.

Reflection must be supposed to have borne fruit in that man of good intellect, who continues to lose, from day to day, all desire for enjoyment.

Yogavasishtha.

Depth such as of the ocean; firmness such as of the *Meru;* and internal coolness such as of the moon;—these arise in the man devoted to *reflection.*

Yogavasishtha.

PART XII.

THE FOUR-FOLD MEANS.

The *four* means of Self-realization beginning with non-attachment, come about from keeping all duties prescribed for the occupation one belongs to; by austerity; and by satisfying God with devotion.

Aparokshanubhuti.

Control; give; sympathize; these three must be learnt and practised: Self-control, charity, and sympathy.

Brhadaranyakopanishad.

Thou longeth after unrealities such as "I" and "mine." Those who *know* wish thy activity were directed to the highest reality. *Thou* never canst know the thing nor can *I*. It is meet, therefore, oh mind! for thee to turn to self-restraint.

Upadesasakasri.

Self-restraint consists in freedom from latent desire. Control consists in checking the activity of the external senses. That is the height of Non-attachment which turns the mind entirely away from the objective. That is the best of Indifference which patiently puts up with all evils whatever. Faith is full confidence in sacred texts and their interpreters. Constant oneness of aim is the mind's fixing on the Eternal Being—this is called Pacification of the mind. Oh my fate! when and how shall I get rid of the bonds of this world—this firm and burning desire may be described as the Desire-for-Liberation.

Aparokshanubhuti.

Where these—Non-attachment and Desire-for-liberation—are as yet in the initial stage, there can but appear a mere glimpse of Self-restraint and the rest, even like a glimpse of water in the mirage.

Vivekachudamani.

The wild mare—Desire—breaking away to the longest distance, and running back as often, keeps roving about up to the very dwelling of the hunters.

Yogavasishtha.

He alone *sees* who looks upon another's wife as upon his own mother; who looks upon another's wealth as upon so much earth and stone; who looks upon every being as upon his own Self.

Smrti.

To the fishes—these men—in the pond of birth and death, wallowing in the slough of the mind, bad latent desires serve for the line to which the woman stands attached as the treacherous bait. He feels desire for enjoyment who has a woman about him; there is no place for enjoyment to the womanless. Abandon woman, and you abandon the whole world; abandoning the whole world, you find supreme happiness.

Yogavasishtha.

Wealth, ever on the move, clouds the intellect, nips the line of virtues in the very bud, and betrays into the net of misery. The man is warm and soft and all that is desirable, to his own and to the world, only as long as he is not sufficiently hardened by wealth, like water by the cold blast.

Yogavasishtha.

Misery attends the acquisition of wealth, and misery attends the protection of wealth acquired, there is misery in its coming, there is misery in its going;—oh! fie upon wealth, the abode of misery out and out.

Panchatantra.

There is no hope of immortality through wealth, and all it may accomplish of good or religion.

Brhadaranyakopanishad.

All growing ends in fading, all rising ends in falling, all meeting ends in parting;—such indeed is the law of this world.

Yogavasishtha.

Oh *Yajnavalkya!* what would your worship mean to the All? which is beyond hunger and thirst, beyond sorrow and illusion, beyond decay and death? It is this Self knowing which, *Brahmans*, renouncing all contact with world, wealth and wife, go about as religious mendicants.

Brhadaranyakopanishad.

Objects of desire, even though they should abide long, are sure to depart. What difference does it make in the *parting*, though men do not part from them of their own accord? This is the answer: If they depart of themselves, they leave immeasurable mental suffering behind; if you part from them they confer on you the endless bliss of self-restraint.

Vairagyasataka.

Death is the law of being. The wise describe it as "Life."

Miscellaneous.

To the really enlightened, this great city—his body—is, like a garden, opening up a passage to liberation through enjoyment; thus all bliss and no pain whatever.

Yogavasishtha.

The mind only half informed, and not yet in full realization of the spotless condition, feels the keenest torture in tearing itself away from objects of enjoyment.

Yogavasishtha.

With every connection which the poor thing binds nearer itself, there is driven an additional spike of harm into its heart of heart.

Mahabharata.

Full of the waters of mental creations; boisterous with the waves of latent desire; infested with the crocodile of attachment; the resort of the birds of imagination; carrying along its mad stream the trees of fortitude growing upon its bank; difficult to cross on account of the treacherous eddies of illusion; enclosed within the impassably high banks of anxiety;—thus supremely terrible runs the river of Desire. The lords of ascetics, with their minds purified of all dross, rejoice in eternal joy, having crossed over to the other side.

Vairagyasataka.

There is the greatest misery in hope, in hopelessness is the height of bliss.

Vairagyasataka.

Everything that depends on Self is bliss, everything that depends on "Self" is misery.

Manu.

A mere cover of bark satisfies one; but another seeks satisfaction in wealth and luxury. The feeling, however, is the same in either case, and the difference is really no difference at all. He, indeed, is the miserable man of poverty who has in him the most insatiable desire. The mind being all contentment, what can make the rich or the poor?

Vairagyasataka.

Oh my heart! to secure what favour dost thou enter this slough of worry and distraction in trying to please the mind of others? If thou wouldst only please thy Self, there would, indeed, dawn of itself, on thee, the power of that jewel which is known to fulfil every desire;—what wish, then, of thine will remain unfulfilled, on the merest thought of the moment?.

Vairagyasataka.

What can be said to the man who finds fault even with him who values at its proper worth all rubbish and its belongings!

Naishkarmyasiddhi.

There is no remedy, within knowledge, which can satisfy each and all. Attend, every way, to thy own good, what can the many-tongued world do to thee?

Jivanmuktiviveka.

When men desirous of doing good, give up even wealth acquired with considerable pains, for the pleasure of others, I would consider it an unmixed good, brought about without any trouble, if men should find satisfaction in speaking ill of me. In this world where we stumble upon poverty of spirit at every step, and which is devoid of every kind of happiness, if any being should find pleasure in speaking ill of me, let him by all means indulge in his feeling, either in my presence or behind my back, for, in this world, all misery, it is very hard to come across even a single moment of such pleasure.

Jnanankusa.

If the wise man of the world who carefully picks holes in the character of others, would but expend the same skill on himself, what could prevent him from breaking through the bonds of Ignorance.

Smrti.

If thou feelest anger at him who does thee the smallest evil, why dost thou not feel anger at the passion itself which entirely spoils the chief aim of existence:—Liberation.

Jivanmuktiviveka.

He who is full of discrimination, who sees one equal Self in friends and foes as well as in himself and can feel no more angry with any one, than with a part of himself.

The Vartika.

Life is as dear to all beings as it is to oneself; feel compassion for every being taking thy own Self as the measure.

Smrti.

Let all be happy; let all enjoy perfect health; let all find the good of their heart; let no one come to grief.

Jivanmuktiviveka.

The triad of the *Veda*, the *Sankhya*, the *Yoga*, the *Pasupata*, the *Vaishnava*;—the three *prasthanas* being interpreted into one or other of these, men look upon *this* as good and upon *that* as agreeable, and so on.—Of men thus betaking themselves to a variety of ways.—straight, easy or difficult,—on account of the difference of intellect, THAT alone is the ultimate resort even like the ocean of all water whatever.

Pushpadantacharya.

The ass carrying a load of sandal-wood is conscious only of the burden, not of the fragrant wood. So, indeed, does he carry about a mere burden who having studied the *Religious Books* knows not their real import and essence.

Uttaragita.

That which is *not* to be, shall never *be;* that which is to *be* shall never *not* be;—why dost thou not drain this draught which will eradicate the poison of anxiety from thyself?

Vairagyasataka.

What means the shaft of love, after youth has gone by? What means the lake, after the water is dried up? What means friends and relatives, after all wealth is gone? What means the world, after the Essence is realized?

S'ankaracharya.

The ascetic with the matted hair; the mendicant with the shaved head; the *Yati* with the hair rooted out; and many others of the same class; play a variety of parts, under the cloth dyed yellow-red.—People though seeing, fail to See, and go through an amount of trouble for the sake of the outward form and show.

S'ankaracharya.

Day follows upon night, evening succeeds morning, the blast of withering cold follows the season full of flowers, and this over and over again. Time plays with the life of beings thus wearing out; and yet the whirl of Desire does never subside.

S'ankaracharya.

One beam meets another in the dash of the great ocean, and becomes immediately separated in the same manner; similar indeed is the meeting of beings with beings.

Mahabharata.

PART XIII.

UNION (YOGA).

Liberation is not on the other side of the sky, nor in the nether world, nor on earth; liberation lies in the mind purified by proper *Spiritual Knowing.*

Yogavasishtha.

He alone is fit to inquire after the *Self*, who has acquired full discrimination; who is firm in non-attachment; who has in him the qualities beginning with self-control; and who, thus qualified, feels keen desire for *knowledge.*

Aparokshanubhuti.

I have studied enough of philosophy, nay I have talked and taught it to my full; And, now I am convinced there is no condition higher than that Silence which comes of the abondonment of all latent desire.

Yogavasishtha.

That is called the highest condition wherein all the five senses and the mind remain under full control and wherein even the intellect does not pass out to other desires. This steadying of the senses is called *Yoga*; the *Yogi* is full awake in that condition, for, *Yoga* is *creating* accompanied with *giving up.*

Kathopanishad.

Firm and studious application to the one Essence, and control of mind;—this is a short statement of the import of "Liberation."

Yogavasishtha.

Two oh Raghava! are the paths leading to suspension,

of *thinking:* *Yoga* which consists in controlling the thinking principle, and Spiritual Knowing which consists in the *proper* eye for experience.

Yogavasishtha.

Yoga is the control of the thinking principle.

Patanjali.

Control of speech; full independence; absence of hope and desire; and constant love of seclusion,—these open the first door to *Yoga.*

Vivekachudamani.

The mind is controlled by practice and non-attachment.

Patanjali.

Spiritual Knowing; control of mind; and destruction of latent desire; these being the reciprocal causes, one of the other, they are the most difficult to accomplish.

Yogavasishtha.

Mind being nearest mind, those who abandoning the true secret, apply themselves only to the body, are described as lost in *physical attachment.*

Yogavasishtha.

Whatever comes to view in this world; whatever raises you to the sky; whatever exalts you to heaven;—everything, oh *Rama!* is within reach after complete destruction of all love and all hate.

Yogavasishtha.

Producing the Self from self, and, as often, deluding self by the Self; inner consciousness leads itself, of its Self, to the bliss of self-realization.

Yogavasishtha.

If *Yoga* consists in restraining the vital breath, this could easily be done through non-attachment, through constant application to the Cause, through some well-conceived device, through the abandonment of evil habits, or through realization of the Absolute.

Yogavasishtha.

Detach thyself from the thing tasted and from that which tastes it, meditate on the *taste alone;* thus *be* ever the Self.

Yogavasishtha.

The mind being full, the whole universe is filled with the juice of nectar; the whole earth is covered with leather to him who has put his foot in the shoe.

Yogavasishtha.

I think those Yogis will never find their efforts sending in any good result, who without knowing spiritual *yoga* address themselves only to physical exercises.

Hathapradipika.

Doing and *suffering* being at end, peace alone survives; —this expanded to the absolute limit, the wise call "liberation."

Yogavasishtha.

Time must elapse between sowing and harvest, nay even in the growth of such wild grass as the holy *Kusa* and the like; *reflection* on the Self ripens into self-realization by degrees, and in course of time.

Panchadasi.

Attach thyself not to *Karma;* but equally attach thyself not to stupid inactivity and suspension of all *Karma* whatever;—*be* what your *are*, equal in all conditions.

Yogavasishtha.

That patience which would empty the ocean drop by drop, at the tip of a straw of the *Kusa*-grass, will, untiringly sustained, establish control over the mind.

Gaudapadacharya.

The inner Self is the *purusha* as big as the man's thumb ever present in the *heart;*—him should he patiently separate from the body like its pulp from the straw.

Kathopanishad.

The One, omnipotent, inner Self of all beings, manifests himself as the manifold. None but those who see Him in themselves, find eternal happiness. Eternal in the eternal; conscious in the conscious; ever one; he sends out all the variety of ideas to all. None but those who see Him in themselves, find eternal peace.

Kathopanishad.

The interval between the mind's passing from one idea to another—the period of calm between the two storms of Thought—may be described as the native condition of Self.

Yogavasishtha.

Fix thy mind on THAT which is not smitten with the evil eye of the Devil of Multifariousness,—causing shakiness of mind.

Yogavasishtha.

What one *does* and what he *thinks*, that he *becomes*.

Brhadaranyakopanishad.

No being ever lives of Air, or Food, or Vitality, but all beings live of the thing that transcends them—of the thing in which they live. I shall explain to thee, once more, the eternal, esoteric Spirit; I shall tell thee, oh Gautama! what becomes of the soul who knows not Spirit after death. Some of these return into the womb of woman for further incarnation, others assimilate themselves with immovable things,—all in accord with the acts they have done, the Idea they have lived.

Kathopanishad.

Neither speech nor mind, nay not even the eye, can realize It; how can It be realized in any category other than Being. It should be realized as pure Being, through proper analysis of both its conditioned and unconditioned *forms*. On him breaks the light of the Essence, beyond Being as well as non-Being, who thus realizes It.

Kathopanishad.

Subject is coloured with object, and object is coloured with subject; both again, are coloured with the sense of "egoism," on the destruction whereof is, therefore, realized the oneness of All.

Naishkarmyasiddhi.

Egoism is plainly not destroyed, till all forms and conventions which hold thee fast in bondage, as in a cage, are annihilated to the extent of leaving absolutely nothing for remainder.

Yogavasishtha.

Being, wisdom, bliss, name, and form, these five make up all objects whatever; the first three make up *Spirit*, the rest the material world.

Drgdrsyaviveka.

Some may cognize the ever blissful, the illuminator of all illumination whatever, even by cognizing It without even these attributes.

Atmapurana.

Said *Yajnavalkya*:—Oh love! the husband is dear not for himself, but for Self; the wife is dear not for herself, but for Self . . . . No one thing is dear for itself, but for Self. This Self should be seen, studied, contemplated, assimilated; oh sweet *Maitreyi!* the study contemplation, and assimilation of Self leaves nothing to know.

Brhadaranyakopanishad.

Said *Yajnavalkya:* It may be seen after the following illustrations: The ocean is the one resort of all water; the skin is the ultimate sphere of all touch; the tongue is the one ground of all taste; the nose is the one basis of all smell; the eye is the one field of all form; the ear is the one place of all sound; the mind is the one source of all ideas; the heart is the one fountain of all knowledge; the Word is the one truth of all the Vedas:—even thus is It the one *fact* of all and every *being*. Put a lump of salt in water, it melts into the water of which it came; you can never grasp it afterwards; it is all salt, every drop of water you may touch. So indeed, oh dear one! is this great, endless unlimited Being,—all thought. The universe coming of this, melts away into this, and being thus lost, loses all distinction whatever.

Brhadaranyakopanishad.

The following may serve for fit illustrations:—When a drum is being beaten it is difficult to catch all the noise that proceeds from it; the drum itself being seen, the whole of the noise that follows the beating is grasped without mistake. When the conch is being blown it is difficult to mark all the sounds that blow themselves out to all directions; the conch being seen the whole of the sound that blows through it is marked without fail. When the lyre is being played upon, it is difficult to observe the notes passing one into the other; the lyre being seen, the music flowing through it is seen in a moment. As from fire fed with wet fuel arise sparks and smoke and the like, so is all this, oh dear one! the mere spontaneous breath of the great *Being*. The *Rigveda*, the *Yajurveda*, the *Samveda*, the *Atharvaveda*, all history, all mythology, all science, all philosophy, all poetry, all aphorisms, all commentaries, all parables;—everything is Its breath.

Brhadarnyakopanishad.

Oh good one! one *form* of clay furnishes the clue to all that is made of clay; all forms and shapes being mere names, mere play of words; the real ground of them all being clay and nothing else. One *form* of gold reveals the nature of all forms of the same metal; all forms being mere names, mere play of words; the real ground of them all being gold and nothing else. One *form* of iron leads to all forms whatever of the same metal; all forms being mere names, mere play of words; the real ground of them all is iron and nothing else. Thus oh good one! should be understood what I explained to thee in the words THOU art THAT. *Chhandogyopanishad.*

Who thinks *the Self* is naught becomes naught; he is all being who knows *the Self* to be.

Taittiriyopanishad.

The whole world is *Spirit*, there is no thing else in Reality;—Betake thyself to this view of things, and rest in peace, thus regaining thy real Self.

Yogavasishtha.

The man attached to "being," is all *being*, through total identification with the Idea; the grub full of the idea of the bee *becomes* the bee.

Vivekachudamani.

Identify the mind with that which leads to good in the end; which is all truth, which is everlasting; which is above illusion; and which is not struck with the eye of evil desire.

Yogavasishtha.

Identification with being leads to *being;* identification with emptiness leads to emptiness; and identification with the All leads to supreme Allness. Study to attain the condition of this Allness.

Aparokshanubhuti.

There is no condition either of bondage or liberation; there is no duality and no unity; it is All-Being—out and out. This is the absolute truth.

Yogavasishtha.

The wise man should fuse all speech and senses into the mind; the mind into the Self that discriminates; the discriminating Self into the great Self; and he should fuse his Self into the Self, all peace and tranquility.

Kathopanishad.

Having destroyed sense with Sense; mind with Mind; egoism with Egoism; I stand supreme as the *Self* of all.

Yogavasishtha.

Use for bow the word of glory, *Aum*, fix the arrow, thy personal Self, on the string; and being all attention, take such unerring aim as will fix the arrow in the target—"*The One Self.*"

Mundukopanishad.

The emptying of the mind of the whole of its illusion, is the true *rechaka* (the process of emptying the lungs of the air they contain); the full realization of the idea "I am *Spirit*" is the true *puraka* (the process of filling the lungs with air drawn in from without); and the firm steady sustenance of the mind on this conviction is the true *Kumbhaka* (the retention of the air inhaled). This is the true *Pranayama* of the enlightened; fools find it only in torturing the nose.

Aparokshanubhuti.

Him death desires to overpower, who wears on his heart the badge of that necklace upon which the vices are held together by the thread of unbroken "latent desires." Death overpowers him whom anger, the fire drying up the waters of discrimination, has power to affect. The oil-mill presses the mixed heap of hard sesamum-seeds into an indiscriminate mass;—death overpowers him, who is similarly pressed by Carnal Lust into a mass, all indiscriminate and confused.

Yogavasishtha.

Arouse the mind if it fall into lethargy! pacify it back into its place if it run out; persuade it by proper knowledge if it tend to the objective;—touch it not when it has found the condition of Peace.

Gaudapadacharya.

Spirituality, the fire which burns up the straw of desire, is all that is meant by the word *Samadhi*, not at all the attitude of silence and contemplation.

Yogavasishtha.

Let the mind function out into the condition beyond distraction; let it, then, take on the form of the idea "I am *Spirit;*" and let it lastly subside into entire forgetfulness of all personality whatever. This is the real ecstasy of the *Saint.*

Aparokshanubhuti.

The absolute sense of universal Being is realized only when consciousness, void of all that it makes conscious, loses itself in the Self, being purified of all relation to personality.

Yogavasishtha.

When all material *thinking* is put out by complete identification with the idea of non-existence, then indeed does consciousness, the common substratum of all, ripen into the absolute sense of universal Being.

Yogavasishtha.

Let Carnal Love and its kind by all means remain for those who still are deluded thereby; Their mere existence can certainly give no offence to the Wise, for the old she-serpent now deprived of her poisonous fangs, is powerless to do any harm to such as these, who have perceived the serpent-nature within her beautiful tinted skin.

Jivanmuktiviveka.

Enjoyment accompanied by Spiritual Knowing conduces to pure contentment. The thief, admitted into company with knowledge of him *as thief*, becomes more a friend than a foe.

Yogavasishtha.

The knower of the Essence, enjoying the pleasures of the senses with moderation, *but knowing them for what they are*, may derive both temporal as well as spiritual pleasure, even like one having knowledge of two languages.

Panchadasi.

I believe him liberated for ever, who performs every

act without the idea of his personally doing it, taking it to be only a part of the multifarious spontaneous action of Nature.

Yogavasishtha.

Fixed abode; desire of fine pots, etc., for use; laying by a store; the taking of pupils; sleeping by day; vain talk;—these six degrade the ascetic into bondage. That ascetic falls in no time who indulges in cohabitation, or who begins to lay by a store of wealth.

Smrti.

The loving woman never ceases to dream of her lover, even when all intent on the discharge of her household duties. The wise finding sweet rest in the supreme undefiled Essence, continue for ever to enjoy it within, though going in the ways of the world, without.

Panchadasi.

Relate thyself not with the future, nor with what has gone by; live the present out with similing heart.

Yogavasishtha.

The consciousness of "self" implied in the "ego," the subject; and the consciousness of "belonging" implied in the "mine" attached to objects;—when both these consciousnesses so to speak are emptied of all content whatever, then indeed does one become the *knower* of Self.

Upadesasahasri.

Thus the *arani*-wood, this self, being constantly worked upon with this other piece of wood, contemplation, there arises the flame of Spirituality burning up all ignorance whatever.

Atmabodha.

He enjoys the ecstasy of absolute bliss, who, in consequence of the absorbing pleasure of Self-realization, rises above all such means as words and objects, and ever stands like the jet of a lamp in some place protected from the breeze.

Drgdrsyaviveka.

The liberated man thinketh ever upon that Being who is the goal of all philosophic reasoning; who is the conviction of every *heart;* who is the All; who is Everywhere; who is Everything.

Yogavasishtha.

He is liberated even against his wish who gains that full consciousness of Self which dispels the illusion identifying Self with the body;—consciousness as strong and firm as that he had while under the illusion.

Upadesasahasri.

Capable of distinguishing good from evil, ever in supreme peace gained through Spirituality, cured of its native restlessness, my mind stands, oh sage! in perfect calm.

Yogavasishtha.

Half of ignorance is destroyed by free exchange of thought; half of the remainder is dispelled by application to philosophy; the rest fades away in the light of Self-reflection.

Yogavasishtha.

Identification with ignorance resulting in obscuration of the light of Self, disappears with the rise of Spirituality.

Panchadasi.

PART XIV.

LIBERATION.

Bow to me, this Self, void of consciousness and that which it makes conscious; void of subject and object, of all names whatever;—Self-illumined for once and for ever. Hail again to me; all rest and peace; the high mountain of supreme bliss, smiling under the sky cleared of all clouds of egoism; fresh after complete extinction of the wild, devastating conflagration of Desire. To the lamp of Love burning bright with its wick of spontaneous ideas without any material oil;—to the light of inner consciousness, the self-sustained sustainer of the intellect and all that depends on it;—right hearty welcome, right joyous greeting!

Yogavasishtha.

Subject, object, instrument, time, space, categories, being, non-being, phenomena, all are *forms* of THAT which is the blessed Self.

Yogavasishtha.

Lightness, health, peace; beauty and grace; melodious voice; profuse fragrance; these signify the first-fruits of *Yoga*. The resplendent ball of gold encrusted with dust, shines in native lustre, when carefully washed; the self having regained its Self shines alone in the eternal bliss of supreme fulfilment.

S'vetas'vataropanishad.

As the sword flashes out of its sheath before the eye in dream, transcending the scheme of all causation; so is the *knower* all Self-effulgent, transcending the five sheaths and standing above all causations.

Upades'asahasri.

Thou mayest realize the distinction between this world and Spirit, to be as like unto the distinction between void and *Ether*.

Yogavasishtha.

Those are the enlightened great souls of this world who happen to be firmly fixed in eternal unborn Calmness. The world can not even dream of it.

Gaudapadacharya.

Sight of the Supreme breaks asunder the knot of egoism in the heart, dispels all doubts, extinguishes all *Karma.*

Mundakopanishad.

The blindest sensualist finds in his mother the irremovable bar to the excess of his indulgence; the man of the sharpest intellect is overcome by the ultimate resort of all thought and all bliss—The One.

Vivekachudamani.

Therefore, the *knower* of The One finishing all learning, should wish to be strong in the Self, and finishing even this strength as well as that learning, he should try to become the silent one. Finishing learning, and strength, and silence, he becomes the true *Brahman*, the real *knower* of *Brahman*. What, indeed, makes the *Brahman?* Whatever may make the *Brahman*, he cannot be other than the one thus described; all beside is vain and worthless.

Brhadaranyakopanishad.

Powder of the *kataka*-wood put into water settles down the mud that makes it foul. So Spirituality constantly put in, drives down the ignorance which renders the soul all turbid, leaving it in the native purity of it-Self.

Atmabodha.

Nothing moves him to love or hate, who finds all beings in himself and himself in all beings. What can delusion or sorrow mean then? when to the *knower* realizing unity of the All, every particle has become his Self.

Isopanishad.

Spiritual Consciousness having shown the absolute non-existence of the objective; the supreme peace of liberation is fully realized in the minds being wiped clean of all and every object whatever.

Panchadasi.

Experience in the light of *Wisdom*, dissolving every impression it may leave behind—this sleep in waking,—is the real nature of those who *know;* liberation is only the highest development of this nature.

Yogavasishtha.

Said *Yajnavalkya:*—This is not the Self, this is not the Self; the incomprehensible is never comprehended; the indissoluble is never dissolved; the unconditioned is never conditioned; the unpained is never pained; never put out;—thou oh *Janaka!* hast realized entire fearlessness.

Brhadaranyakopanishad.

The bliss of *Brahman!*—speech and mind fall back baffled and abashed; all fear vanishes in the *knowing* of that bliss.

Taittiriyopanishad.

The silent one, the *knower* ever resting in the Self, may walk, stand, sit, lie down, or do anything at his sweet will.

Vivekachudamani.

I do not see, for, I have no eyes; without ears, how can I hear? I cannot speak, for, I have no speech; without mind how could I find the world of mind?

Upadesasahasri.

There is none superior to me in Self-knowledge, none inferior to me in ignorance; who knows thus, is the greatest *knower* of *Brahman.*

Naishkarmyasiddhi.

Neither knowable nor unknowable; neither spoken nor unspoken; neither liked nor disliked; impossible of retaining in any mental presentation; nay not possible to fix in contemplation even for a moment; all bliss through and through; beautiful in the deep sense of ecstatic self-realization; this my-Self wonderfully dissolves the world in the sudden flash of its abundant light.

Svarajyasiddhi.

Separate, unique, one, multifarious, knowable, knower, motive, mover,—these and other imaginings of the same kind, where could they find room other than in me all One?

Upadesasahasri.

Egoism having disengaged itself from the body, and having been dissolved in the light of Supreme Self, the mind stands in a blissful state wherever it goes, whatever it directs itself to.

Drgdrsyaviveka.

The native form of the subject, highly transcendent, self-illumined for once and for ever, unborn, one, immutable, unconditioned, all-pervading, without a second;—I am this, the ever liberated word of glory.

Upadesasahasri.

He has had a dip in the holy waters of all sacred rivers; he has given the whole earth in pious gift; he has offered a thousand sacrifices; he has satisfied all the gods in heaven; he has lifted his ancestors out of the circle of birth and death; he deserves worship of all the three worlds;—the man whose mind has, even for a moment, tasted of peace in the absorbing idea of *Brahman.*

Miscellaneous.

Neither love nor hate; neither ambition nor illusion; neither pride nor the least tinge of jealousy; no good, spiriutal or temporal; no desire; no liberation;—I am none of these, I am all Bliss, the Bliss of All Eternal Consciousness. Holiness or unholiness; happiness or misery; incantation or holy pilgrimage; scripture or sacrifice; none of these belong to me; not even the enjoyed, the enjoyer, or the sense of enjoyment; I am all Bliss, the Bliss of All Eternal Consciousness. Death I fear not; caste I respect not; father, mother, nay even birth, I know not; relatives; friends I recognize not; teacher and pupil I own not;—I am all Bliss, the Bliss of All Eternal Consciousness.

S'ankaracharya.

I am *Brahman,* not at all of the world, never apart from *Brahman;* I am not the body, nor have I any body whatever;—I am the unconditioned, eternal One.

S'ankaracharya.

Who, being full of unity, sees not, as in sleep, the least trace of duality, though seeing it in entire wakefulness; who though acting is, for the same reason, entirely at rest;—he and no one else is verily the true knower of Self.

Upadesasahasri.

He is all taste and refinement, yet all insipid; He is merciless, yet fondness itself; He is cruel, yet all compassion; He is beyond desire, yet deep in the whirl of all desire. All care and anxiety without, like the rest of Mankind,—yet all quiet and calm within, He stands as if possessed, though ever unpossessed.

Yogavasishtha.

Regaling all content in the nectar of *Bliss;* fully satisfied in superme fulfilment of every duty; there remains nothing for the *yogi* to do; if anything remain, he must be just so many removes hehind *Bliss.*

Jivanmuktiviveka.

The least of a thing is greatest if it comes without trouble to any one; without seeking it of the wicked; and without the least pang at heart.

Mahabharata.

The cycle of strife and struggle will place *Brahman* in the mouth of all. None, oh *Maitreya!* will know it, if intent on the pleasures of sex and stomach.

Jivanmuktiviveka.

I am *Brahman,* I am the Creator;—those who do not thus know me, are lost to Wisdom as also to the purifying forms of external worship;—they are on the highway to materialistic Atheism.

Upades'asahasri.

Oh *Gargi!* who performs the sacrifice; who undergoes the severest penance even for several thousands of years; all without knowledge of this Immutable Essence, meets only with that good which is sure to end. Who passes away, dear *Gargi!* from this world, without knowledge of this Immutable Essence, goes away, alas! with the tight bond of narrowness about his heart; he alone who passes away in the knowledge of this Immutable Essence is the real *Brahman.*

Brhadaranyakopanishad.

The heart of the wicked never melts into goodness, even though he should be deep immersed in the *Vedanta.*

Jagannath.

Always at their best while talking of *Brahman,* but without the heart having at all *become* It, being all coloured with love of the world;—these too, are ignorant fools of the first degree, never free from the circle of death and birth.

Aparokshanubhuti.

Who does *not* know, *knows;* who *knows,* does *not* know; It is *known* to those who do *not* know, It is *not* known to those who *know.*

Kenopanishad.

The ladle helps to prepare a variety of viands, but it never knows the taste of any one of them: he knows all the four *Vedas*, and Institutes of Duty without end, but the poor thing knows not the essence of them all—*Brahman*.

Uttaragita.

Attachment to any one of the many fields which the mind visits for exercise, is the surest sign of ignorance; greenness is certainly impossible in the tree that conceals a consuming fire in its hollow.

Naishkarmyasiddhi.

The swimmer, having safely carried many to the other side of the stream, is drawn into the whirlpool, and is carried beyond all help. Those, on the other side, who feel grateful for his help, pity him, others pass on in indifference. The Wise Man caught into the whirlpool of words and technicalities, has the pity of those who having reached the other side of all words and all forms feel yet grateful for his help.

Atmapurana.

That knower of Self who yet deals in "give and get returns" hath not graduated himself for Liberation.

Upades'asahasri.

The wise grieve not, having seen the unbodied Self pervading all mortal forms, ever great, all-embracing.

Kathopanishad.

As is the being of things; the void-ness of void; or the being with forms of forms; so is this Universe. That whereof comes the whole universe at the end of sleep, and that wherein it dissolves itself at the moment of rest, is this *chidakasa*.

Yogavasishtha.

The area of this cosmos can hardly suffice for the enjoyment of the high-minded knower; the flutter of a tiny fish can produce but a scant ruffle on the surface of the deep.

Bhartrhari.

Though taking part in all affairs of every kind, like all ordinary men, he soars constantly above all beings, conscious or unconscious.

Yogavasishtha.

If one knows his self as the Self, what desire, what object, should burn bis body in the fever of care and anxiety.

Brhadaranyakopanishad.

Think of It, speak of It, enlighten one another in It;—this is full devotion to the idea of Oneness, this, the wise call study of *Brahman.*

Panchadasi.

The irrevocable love which the indiscriminate have in objects of sense;—may that very love never fade from my heart while it yet continues to be full of thy holy memory.

Panchadasi.

Great souls, ever at rest in the Self, all light and standing at the height of development, are always as firm within as mount Meru, though appearing as fickle without as the tip of a feather.

Yogavasishtha.

Neither joy nor sorrow; neither movable nor immovably fixed; neither being nor non-being; nay not even the intermediate between these opposites;—so is described the mind of the enlightened.

Yogavasishtha.

The army engaged in close battle, in a picture, fights all unmoved; the wise, though deep in intercourse with the world, stands equally even in all conditions.

Yogavasishtha.

The Vedas; the constant study of the *Scriptures;* close application to the subleties of philosophy;—what do these avail! What, indeed, is the use of that whirl of ceremonial worship, which at best lodges the weary soul in some hovel of the village called Heaven! Conscious harmony in the blissful condition of Self, the great-*pralaya*-fire destroying the net of misery born of the bondage of this world;—all, saving this, are but the toys of spiritual pedantry.

Bhartrhari.

The Soul imagining itself into the act, takes on the result of that act; not imagining itself into the act, it is ever free of the result.

Yogavasishtha.

Where could THAT be invoked which fills all space? where is the seat of THAT which is the seat of all? Of the Pure, what can be the wash or the offering of honour?—what the drink that purifies within?

S'ankaracharya.

I have no distraction, and therefore no attraction; distraction or attraction are all incidents of the mind under power of attraction.

Upades'asahasri.

The idea which consciousness, at first, imagines, of itself, as its own form, *that* it continues to *be* even to the present day. The same consciousness may, by yet another effort of greater strength, take the opposite form, and so on and on, in proportion to the effort it should put forth.

Yogavasishtha.

Neither teacher nor book, neither pupil nor teaching, neither you nor I, neither this nor that;—the light of Self, intolerant of all doubt whatever, I am all pure bliss, the one *residuum* of the many thus denied.

S'ankaracharya.

The patient *Brahman* having known It should harmonize himself in the Self, he should not be deluded away by words; it is mere waste of breath.

Brhadaranyakopanishad.

The wise having found the path of *Wisdom* indirect and direct, from the study of books, should then cast them away even like straw after threshing the rice out of it.

Panchadasi.

This is the truth: I know no change, for, there can be no cause to change, there being all Oneness out and out. No spiritual merit or demerit, no liberation or bondage, nor have I any *caste or locality*, for, I have not the body of which these are accidents.

Upades'asahasri.

None of the philosophies do I profess; I am that pure consciousness, the subject of distinct Self-experience; all pure bliss; the one *residuum* of the many thus denied.

S'ankaracharya.

In the duties of *Caste* and *Neighborhood* some take delight; in child-like innocence, some in stupid indifference, others find their meed; lover, reveler, ascetic, to no one grade of life the *knower* confines his choice.

Svarajyasiddhi.

A perfect fool in one place, all royal splendour in another; at times in fond delusion, at times entire peace and quiet; often in the slothful indifference of the boa; the subject of the highest encomiums in one place, in another all contempt; in a third entirely unnoticed;—thus goes about the wise knower, ever happy in the highest bliss.

Vivekachudamani.

The ascetic, not straying away from the path of wisdom, should so conduct himself that foolish men, feeling ill at ease, should seek not his company.

Smrti.

The ignorant set up this panorama of objects, I wipe it out as often; I have faith in none; I am not afraid of the last penalty; I hate so-called virtue; Self-satisfaction is all I seek. The whole of my wonderful life spent in escaping the World, none can understand.

Svarajyasiddhi.

What means Self-realization to me, all eternal realization from end to end; all duties have been done, all wishes have been fulfilled, this is the most sure conviction of my heart.

Panchadasi.

I neither do nor make do, I neither enjoy nor make enjoy, I neither see nor make see; I am the self-effulgent Self unlike every possible name or form.

Vivekachudamani.

The knower and the ignorant are both equally subject each to his own previous *Karma;*—the knower, all patience, knows no sorrow; the ignorant, ever unsteady, continues to grieve. Of two men passing on the road, both being equally fatigued and the road before them being equal, he that knows treads on patiently to the end, the poor ignorant fool lingers behind bemoaning his lot.

Panchadasi.

Bliss here attends the extremes of Intellect;—the highest which transcends Intellect, and the lowest which is far below Intellect. The way between these extremes is the way of worry and evil. A very thin partition divides ecstasy from madness; for, in the former, the mind having lost all faith is quite clear of every tinge of attachment.

Yogavasishtha.

In all acts whatever, whether of commission or omission, there is nothing, save absence of attachment, to distinguish the fool from the man of wisdom.

Yogavasishtha.

I look with equal eye upon a poisonous snake or a garland of flowers; upon a strong enemy or a kind friend;

upon a costly jewel or a lump of earth; a bed of flowers or a slab of stone; a group of beautiful women or a collection of useless straw;—thus do I spend all my days in some holy solitude, all intent on the blissful syllable.

Bhartrhari.

Neither action nor inaction are in me, ever one and without parts; how can he act who is all one Self, a compact mass, all-full and all-filling like the *Ether?*

Vivekachudamani.

He is never overjoyed though often coming to good things; he stands firm as Meru under the direst calamity; he walks the world like a god, finding Self in the bliss of Self in everything whatever.

Svasajyasiddhi.

A *Chandala;* a twice-born; a *S'udra;* an ascetic; a man of intellect refined by application; the lord of *Yogis;* —thus described at the top of thoughtless prattle by men conceiving each his own fancy, sages harmonized in the Self wend their way neither angry nor proud of the compliments thus bestowed.

Bhartrhari.

The knower catches in the ecstasy of his heart the full light of that *Brahman* which is indescribable, all thought, all pure bliss, incomparable, transcending time, ever free, beyond desire, resembling limitless *Ether,* having no parts and admitting of no idea beside itself.

Vivekachudamani.

Does it make any difference in this gem of heaven, the sun, if he is reflected in the waters of the Ganges or in the stream flowing through the scavenger's street? Does it make any difference in the *Ether* enclosed in an earthenware or in a jar of gold? In THAT, the inner being of all, the billowless ocean of native bliss and light, what means this great delusion, this nightmare of separateness, creating distinctions? The self-same Self shines plainly in all the three conditions of waking, dream and sleep; it is, moreover, the inner witness of all,—pervading even like a thread, all forms whatever from *Brahma* to the tinniest ant;—He who has the firm conviction "I am this Self," not the form it takes, let him be a *Brahman* or *a low-caste*, my mind points to him as the real Master.

S'ankaracharya.

Has it set? is it broken? is it shattered to pieces? is it dissolved? is it pounded to dust? is it swallowed up? is it suddenly gone to decay?—the mind being turned inward, I do not find even a trace of the universe in the free depths of myself, the indescribable ocean of the bliss of Self-realization.

Svarajyasiddhi.

All latent desire having died out, he looks upon the world as all destroyed; as some unreal nightmare; as a castle-in-the-air; or even as a painting which is nearly washed off under a heavy downpour of rain.

Yogavasishtha.

Though ever moving about in the world of experience, the whole of it exists not for him;—all-pervading ether-like consciousness alone subsists. Such a one is called *Liberated.* The expression of his countenance neither flushes nor fades under pleasure or pain; he stands unmoved whatever may come or go. Though acting after every feeling, such as love, hate, fear and the like, he who stands unaffected within, is said to be the liberated while yet in this life. He whom the world finds no cause to fear, and who is never afraid of the world, ever beyond joy, and jealousy, and fear, is said to be the real *Liberated One.* With the woes of this world laid entirely, at rest he who, though full of all learning and art, is yet without any; who, though with mind is without it, is said to be the real *Liberated One.*

Yogavasishtha.

Trembling and other signs of fear subside, only by degrees, even after knowledge of the snake as nothing but a harmless piece of rope; the same rope met with in dim light, even after such knowledge, may yet become the same terrible snake it once was. Thus previous *Karma* comes gradually to end by fruition through experience and not all at once by any obstinate remedy; nay, it is even possible for the immortal one to temporarily feel his mortality in moments of such fruition. This, however, is no flaw in the condition of *Spirituality* once realized, for, *Liberation* is no observance, it is being at harmony with the course of nature.

Panchadasi.

When all desires infesting the heart are entirely given up, the mortal becomes immortal and lives in *Spirit* even here. The slough cast off by the serpent lies dead and lifeless on the ant-hill; so even lies this body; and the mortal, who is thus disembodied, while yet here, becomes immortal, all life, all *Spirit*, all light.

Brhadaranyakopanishad.

The highest Self, all endless bliss, unconditioned limitless consciousness, being realized, whether through the great texts, or through *Yoga*, in all experience whatever, let one lose himself in the ecstasy of Realization, for he has for ever lost all touch with bondage of every description.

Svarajyasiddhi.

Clad in rich cloth or in the wide expanse of space, having his skin alone for cover, or buried deep in the ample folds of all-embracing thought,—he wanders the world like a madman,—like a child, or even like a ghost, when compared with the unfolded of his race.

Vivekachudamani.

Without having in one's self the clear light of Self-experience, no one can appreciate the phenomenal sublimity of another's experience in the same line.

Yogavasishtha.

As timber is carried away by the stream to places high and low, so even is the body led by Law to whatever awaits it at its proper time.

Vivekachudamani.

The traveller with mind firmly fixed only on the goal he is approaching, never feels the motion of his legs along the road he treads; act thus in all you do.

Yogavasishtha.

The fright caused by the appearance of a thief survives his capture, the cloth yet leaves the impress of its form on the ashes to which it is burnt;—the world reduced of itself to naught in the case of the Knower, lasts with his body to bear out such fruition as previous *Karma* should bring.

Svarajyasiddhi.

The knower may, oh child! let his external senses manifest in acts and all conditions as long as his body lasts; but he should never let his internal sense go with the external.

Yogavasishtha.

The *Ether* may appear in any condition whatever, it is never conditioned. The Self never takes on the properties of whatever accidents may appear to colour his Self.

Atmabodha.

The knowers of the Supreme neither avoid nor court intercourse with the world, they go with whatever should turn up in ordinary course. "Being in all, I am ever inactive," he who, with this conviction, acts in accord with what is brought to him in the course of nature is always inactive. He is not motionless though standing; he does not walk though going; he is all peace though deep in intercourse; he is ever inactive though full of activity.

Yogavasishtha.

This kind of apparent "latent desire" in those who have found liberation while living is no desire at all; it is that universal sense of *being* which is known as pure being.

Yogavasishtha.

Having known It thus, fill thyself with the memory of pure Unity; having realized the Unit, walk the world like a mass of so much dead matter. No praise, no salute, no offerings even to the dead, no fixed or unfixed abode,—the harmonized soul should ever live in Faith and Trust.

Gaudapadacharya.

The fifteen rays return into their source; the divine forces governing the senses find back the universal fountain of their rise; the reflection in the inner sense—the embodied soul—together with every action whatever, all become one in the supreme unchangeable Essence. As rivers flowing into the ocean lose their individual name and form, nay thus lose even themselves, so does the *knower*, freed from all name and all form, find the highest Being, all light. He who thus *knows* the highest *Self*, verily becomes *Self;* none that is born in his family has his eye closed to *Self*. He soars above sin and sorrow; freed from the ties of the heart, he becomes immortal.

Mundakopanishad.

Giving up the body in some holy place or in the house of *the lowly*, conscious or unconscious, he finds *Liberation*, all cause of sorrow being entirely destroyed, and liberation being found in the very moment of the rise of *Spiritual Consciousness*.

Vartika.

Water is water, whether it stands all placid or surges up in high billows; it makes no difference to the Ocean. Embodied or disembodied, there is no difference in the liberation of the silent knower. What difference can embodiment or disembodiment make in the Liberated? Whether in tempestuous waves or in placid calm, the sameness of Ocean undergoes no change.

Yogavasishtha.

Who has no desire, who is beyond desire, who has all desires fulfilled in the Supreme, who has Self as the object of all and every desire;—his breath rises not beyond him; being *Self,* he becomes *Self,* in truth.

Brhadaranyakopanishad.

I have no Illusion for my consort; no serpent for my couch; no discuss for my weapon; no round of incarnations to go through, nor have I the anxiety of protecting the world, still I am the Lord, to all intent and purpose, in my Self.

Svarajyasiddhi.

The *Absolute* neither rises nor sets, nay he is never laid at rest. He is not *being* nor non-*being,* neither near nor distant, neither I nor thou. He shines as the sun, He protects the three worlds appearing as *Vishnu,* As *Sira* He destroys all. He acts the creator in the form of the lotus-born *Brahma.* Whatever is, whatever has been, whatever shall be,—every object in any one of the three forms of Time—He is that; He is everything. Oh best of knowers! when He takes on the form of the three worlds and all they contain, I believe Him to have gone through the act of creation. If verily the three worlds do exist, let him by all means become those words, for *in* Him the "Three worlds" are, in truth, empty of all real content whatever—mere words are they?

Yogavasishtha.

They divert themselves in the native bliss of Self-experience, they enjoy themselves in any manner with perfect freedom. The many-sided, wonderful course the Liberated pursue, on the inscrutable Path, ever free of attachment, knowing no limit, always tending to the good of the universe, is as inscrutable as the course of fishes in water, the passage of birds in the atmosphere, or the course of wind throughout space.

Svarajyasiddhi.

Doubt, dispute and explanation, all depend on language which means duality. In the language of Unity, there can be no question and no answer.

Panchadasi.

There is in Reality no dissolution, no creation, none in bondage, no pupilage, none desirous of liberation, none liberated;—this is the Absolute Truth.

Gaudapadacharya.

Bow to him who enunciated this method of harmony in the Absolute, conducing to the well-being of all, beneficent, above all dispute, entirely at One.

Gaudapadacharya.

Wonderful, supremely wonderful—this Philosophy! More wonderful still the Masters who teach the Truth! A thousand wonders surround the depth of *Spiritual Consciousness* taught! The bliss of Knowledge is the Silence of indescribable wonder!

Panchadasi.